THE BLUE MIMES

Winner of the 2023 Academy of American Poets First Book Award

Selected by Eduardo C. Corral

Sponsored by the Academy of American Poets,
the First Book Award is given annually to the winner of an open competition
among American poets who have not yet published a book of poems.

THE BLUE MIMES

Poems

SARA DANIELE RIVERA

Graywolf Press

This publication is made possible, in part, by the voters of Minnesota through a Minnesota State Arts Board Operating Support grant, thanks to a legislative appropriation from the arts and cultural heritage fund. Significant support has also been provided by other generous contributions from foundations, corporations, and individuals. To these organizations and individuals we offer our heartfelt thanks.

Published by Graywolf Press
212 Third Avenue North, Suite 485
Minneapolis, Minnesota 55401

www.graywolfpress.org

Published in the United States of America

ISBN 978-1-64445-279-0 (paperback)
ISBN 978-1-64445-280-6 (ebook)

2 4 6 8 9 7 5 3 1
First Graywolf Printing, 2024

Library of Congress Control Number: 2023940113

Cover design: Mary Austin Speaker

Cover art: Sara Daniele Rivera

In honor of all the beloved we've lost.

In every confluence of light.

Contents

I

II

III

THE BLUE MIMES

I

No cierra una herida una campana. Una campana no cierra una herida.

Close a wound a bell cannot. A bell cannot close a wound.

—Alejandra Pizarnik

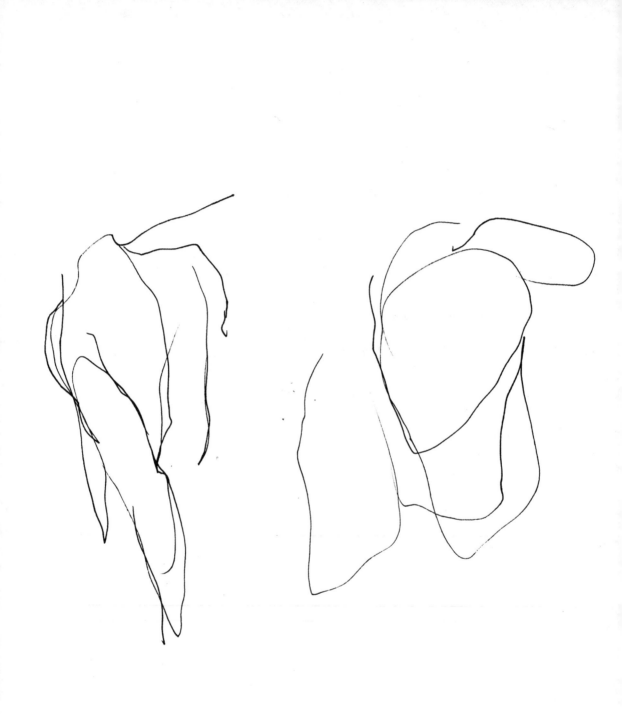

Earthworks

June 2021

Now it's all
erased: a black stone
polished by water.

[Contained wreckage. Silence in the empty plaza. The house broken and split.
A table set with blanks.]

Mom drips Holy Water onto the roots
of the two-thirds-dead catalpa tree. I'm sorry,
give it one more spring,   our hearts were miles away

while you were dying. You were dying

while our hearts traveled
root-pathways to arrive inside
the tiniest chamber inside

the last galón de oxígeno we could get to Surco.

We couldn't save what was far from us. We couldn't save what was near.

I spent a winter poised
on fine-drawn lines

of disaster, thinking I'd already lost
          my six spiders, things I held tender

in my mouth as I slept. The thinness of a heart stops and it is the thinness of a leg, too
small to make any sound when it separates.

When I find what I've lost on the ground I think
it's an eyelash. Then I think, no,

it's an obliteration. We have violently failed each other.

[The gut hovers where it isn't supposed to be. So wind moves under the kale leaves.]

I'm trying to believe
we were earthworks together, a spiral seam,

division between earth and snow,

leaves of one color bleeding
        into leaves of another.

                [Into the memory of Spanish mass as the choir starts "Vienen
                con alegría" and I leave and call you with the music of my
                childhood trailing me up the hill and you're alive and ask
                where I am because you never remember how far I am from
                you. Y cuando me vienes a ver. Aquí tu sabes que nunca voy
                a ningún sitio.]

The absence, always there, echoes inside
        delineations of light. It becomes a boulder

                suspended in the branches of
                a coppiced tree. A silence at the center
                of a fracture. Red ombre cradling
                a void. A swell of
                burnished gold.

                        [For you a hundred hand-drawn lighthouses.

                                A hundred painted little boats.]

Someone curls into themselves at
the edge of the sea. At the edge

of the sea I lose one corner
of my kindness, almost lose

you. When we have to heal
we walk spirals, speak into wind.

Keep the lost parts of me where
your body becomes castle,
in the dark without edge.

I do not want my old skin.
I do not want anything it wanted.

Al borde del mar alguien está
acurrucada. Al borde del mar

pierdo un rincón de mi
amabilidad; casi te pierdo.

Cuando hay que sanar caminamos
en espirales, hablamos al viento.

Guarda mis partes perdidas donde
tu cuerpo se vuelve castillo,
en la oscuridad sin borde.

No quiero mi piel antigua.
No quiero nada de lo que quería.

Keys

In a dream, a dream you wrote
down, you open a door,

the architecture similar
to your island town only

there are curves where you knew
something other than curves.

The colors you search for
have changed, softened over

time, all those stones dropped
through the chambers of your body—what

does it mean to have survived that—

what can you do now with
all your collected keys—

In a memory, a memory you
wrote down, you eat stolen

mango in the sepia
of a photograph, the day everyone in

your family wore the same color
without planning it, but film

couldn't capture that
particular miracle—

hit a stick against the trunk
of memory and everything
comes shaking down.

There is a reality you try to catch.
A door that fits, colors that speak
of safety, to no longer be falling inside

yourself and have others call it
                    survival—

The last thing you wrote down is the last thing
that made you laugh: that woman, la sin vergüenza

slapped by her man in the middle
of the street, how she turned

y así, jua, yanked
his pants to his ankles—

She is the stone that sits in
your diaphragm. All you're left with
is a stone in your diaphragm,

as you back from the page
get up from the table
and walk through the door.

January

There must be some advantage to the light.
    —Maurice Riordan

Our minds conceive the end
of something, then conceive

the beginning. A highway overpass extends
forward and back but

it's the framing that matters. Am I
healing or forgetting. Am I
happy or a little less terrified.

The year began with insurrection at the Capitol.
A swarm. Worrisome dead bees.

Mom fixated on the windows: How can you just break
those windows, she asked. How can you just

climb up to those windows and break them—

The year began with a reminder
that we are at a flexion point,
midpath in darkening dusk,

blockades of hollow-veined flowers,
lawmakers tweeting from the caverns
of escape hoods.

Maybe there is no direction from here.
Only recognition of light posts

studding the road, terror broken
by intervals of hope.

Which must give some advantage, right?
Which must illuminate us forward or back.

multi-nights

i locate the love void & yet, / i know all is well.
  —Juan Felipe Herrera

the first time i
failed you i cooked
something inedible
asked if our hands
lacked something
evolutionary
that we can't know
the beaches
our fathers have forgotten
what people used to eat
en el malecón
their knees propped
and where were you
when we broke
like bread
together
la comida mal hecha
where were you
when your
father's world
ended
probably driving
down espejo street
mirándote
in the rearview
una mirada
my mother says
you can always
tell with people
cara de bueno
cara de malo
i slept for years
in half a bed

where were you
probably climbing
a lover like a watchtower
and do you remember
at the peak
seeing the whole
of a broken city
each window a smokestack
saran-wrapped
for cold even that
una cosa mal hecha
that crumbled like
a foreclosure
a la vez
una cosecha
the songs of childhood mass
were all songs of harvest
of walking barefoot
even in the desert
and if you
could have known who
in your life would desert you
before cooking them dinner
what would you choose
to burn

The Split

At eleven years old I
followed you down
a path you knew

from your father's
place, over a footbridge,
dodging the cholla

and nopales.
Boulders rose,
tilting together

in the climbing
elevation of
the mountain.

We chose a flat-faced
boulder, a lookout west
over the city

where everything tapered
away. At the far end
of the horizon we could

trace the low blue line
of the Sangre de Cristos.

Between us, another
line, a split

down the center
of the rock.

•

Year to year the graffiti
changes. Two halves
of the rock become

the halves of a broken
heart. Months later, the
halves say FU CK.

Those were the
splitting days.
The jigsaw of

my body didn't fit.
I'd stand in front
of the mirror pinching

my arms, seeing only
my arms, my arms
disconnecting

like horrible wings from
my body. One arm, a bat.
The other arm, an owl,

lifting away but
closing in as on Goya's
body in sueño.

Reason sleeps
for girls that age.
Monsters don't.

●

We took a picture standing
on either side of the crack.
Ten years later, the same

picture, only more
had been rubbed away.

We wore white-and-green
dresses, took each other's
forearms for

balance. Broken bottles
gleamed through gravel
shadow.

We needed
to walk an uneven line

away from our bodies,
needed a place

where Goya's crows could
become illusions,

because we'd had
our share of crows

and weren't always able
to protect the gaps.

•

And so, between us,
there are bad days, days

we forget but carry
anyway, an extra weight
on the body.

But you are also
my footbridge leading to

the other days, when
I remain wholly

myself and the earth rebuilds
itself and what I leave

behind inscribed
is how much I love you and

the dividing lines

I would walk
to be able to say it.

Rompecabezas

Twin girls no one is looking for walk, their hands tracking walls of contiguous houses. Their hands drip with remains of cremoladas and they are all possibility: future siblings, parents who will also die young. A cream church rings them in shadow. El Misti drapes them long in shadow. They are volcano-children, daughters of Arequipa, they erupt or they sleep. They run hot into the gray specter of the ocean.

Sunray yuccas. Barrel-bodies under the clouded sun. Their clothes get stolen on the beach. This happens sometimes, you go swimming and someone takes your clothes so you turn home having lost something having gained something, living contact, salt-skin to air, the shame and the perfection. Skin pricks into a starmap. Right then it's exhilarating to have no one and nothing

protecting you. One girl stops, mira, mira, she says, scanning the bareness of a plaza. It's only her, she realizes, her twin died at birth, one piece of the composition lifts away rompecabezas the shape of a sister goes blank and a dreamscape unmakes itself and the remaining girl her head splits open on impact because who knows when the earth started shaking, it has always been shaking, this has always been the most tremulous grounds for a story. She's torn from time the moment the wall collapses. Generations later no one is looking for her name. There remains the scaffold of a plot, a rent seam in the sky.

summer at taos

for Dad

what we find
as we drive in is a fissure
that tracks flat
ground like a scar

an expanse of granite
& cloud long enough
to match the vowels in a word—

what was it
the word we saw fifty miles back on a highway overhang
      the one we couldn't pronounce

•

is a chasm of starlight
what you envisioned

is that what ripped
the earth & everything apart

        actual stars
     pulled down from star-filled skies
     to rest like adornment on rock

i hold a spiral fossil
in my palm
in my palm also i can fit

       the breakage of a gorge
     the vision of you as you drive

i tell you the fossil is called *feather star*
the night sky can stay where it is

●

     you & i
learned to identify
fossil & geode together

but on that day i wasn't watching
the ground i was watching you

i was watching the calliopes
sonation of tail & wing & theirs

was also a name i whispered

my mouth wanting to learn
the character of *o* & *i*

●

we pry open
what we know of each other

how far we can drive without
disjuncture

(if we have disjuncture let it be beautiful
     as two unexpected textures
     adobe & rusted wire
     green chile beer
aluminum on cold green water)

●

what we once protected
we expose

the west
wall of a canyon at daybreak

you speak to me in strips of light
in words i can pronounce
you are what i find & what i found

along the road
in the tumbled shadowed white

& you who gave me a name you
give me a turn

    let me drive out
at night starlight
                    in every breach

Resound

for Isaac

What if on that same highway, the whole city
skirting east, you could become a sound. Lost

for hours, the echo dusk. The canyon of your mind
filling in everything that might have been

written. Our time fragments together, yellow, white,
dusted black, heaps of beargrass but I

suspend us in a single car ride. You were driving
the Tacoma. To me it was always as if you

had walked up from dewed shadow, from
another story of the world and when

you talked pecan trees, points of intersection
where deserts meet, it was like hearing names

reinvented. I want to believe now that you
can see in multiplicities, the ultimate fire tower,

that you can see this controlled burn
and as everything blackens seedlings spill from

a rust-colored pinecone, breach the smoke
and grow. You become a progressive tense, alive

in a memory as in the juncture of a moment. A new
pattern of *listening to hear*

where you are. To hear the music of a wind
current, moving west over water.

Quilla

A silver-blue star at the bottom of a glass. A blood spot:
        something shed from the body

transforms, crawls away on red wire legs. A dark stain
        blossoms on your face, tunnels inward and becomes

a blankness in your brain. Border between tonalities
        of skin. I press your body to

my face mid-ascension, reasoning we were never human,
        always foxes holding too hard to our sources

of protection. Darkening can be a trace of love. In a dust storm
        darkening can be a loss of

dimensionality. In the before of our family
        twin sisters died, one at birth the other

something to do with an earthquake. Nameless halves of a swept unit.
        Salt left midair. Silver and silver and silver

the teardrops flood their containment. I skip stones at the edge
        of Callao, sling language across the blue: I knew

you, I wish I knew you. A plane of water dazes
        after a stone has sunk.

I have begged the animal inside me to release
        its captive light. I have hurled this

toward you out of silence, attempting contact
        with what I will never

touch. A body lodged
        behind an eclipse.

Sonnet to Sleep Paralysis

after John Keats

It began for us, hushed, that year. You and I insisted
on seeing each other then sat slack with the unsayable.
Retreat to separate apartments, mirror our way across
rooms, night birds singing as the world folded itself
and stained us like two halves of a Rorschach. When
we woke we were not butterflies, not people. Only
the center of a cleaving. Mine was an old woman in
the corner: Bisabuela, I was sure. Would she leave me
alone, please, out of love? Knitting dread, yours against
your chest, a saddled demon barreling black. This is the
language our minds create when we hold everything
back. Identical vaults. *You need each other*, the
phantom says. *Que no se les olvide*, says Bisabuela
through the transparency of her head.

II

Two thousand feet high we were,
suspended between sky and water,
aware only of our heads.

Estábamos a dos mil pies de altura,
suspendidos entre el cielo y el agua,
conscientes solo de nuestras cabezas.

—Mario A. Rivera

Abrigar

verbo transitivo / transitive verb

A lullaby opens a rift, and in comes the cold. *Los pollitos dicen pío pío pío cuando tienen hambre cuando tienen frío—*

When you sang in Spanish you carved space for us within language. The hollow under a wing. The texture of a word vibrates, *acurrucaditos*. The moment of shifting and turning over into sleep.

Cubrir el cuerpo con ropa para protegerlo del frío o evitar que se enfríe.

Shifting and turning into sleep my sister's breath is light, rattling. We fit on a twin daybed each in one of Dad's arms. In unfamiliar landscapes her breath is the only signal that nothing is coming.

On the worst night of our lives every mattress tunnels, doubles as if meeting a mirror, never to return to the anchor of the body. I wake to see my sisters holding each other on the floor. I hold this moment between two fingers, like a boulder suspended between the walls of a gorge.

Cover the body with clothes to protect it from cold or keep it from getting cold.

To protect someone: a seam, wing, rising chest, incense, luminaria. Try not to be a bad association.

Try to be a light source held in a window and when people walk past at night they might feel nostalgic without knowing what's going on inside. Break me open and the light is warm. My body is a containment field, skin under skin under skin, a perpetual process of layering.

Baudelaire wrote that winter enhances the poetry of the house. When the out-of-doors cold is an external frame and our interiors protected. But the body on its own is a vulnerable house. Take away the walls, the set pieces, the stucco that meets the sidewalk, and there's only the body trying to guard whatever light it can.

Resguardar o proteger a alguien o algo de una temperatura baja o de las inclemencias del tiempo.

There's only the body, only the little glass box shattered and reshattered, complicated by its own shards. The world we thought we knew, the country we thought we could belong to.

It's the night of the election, the moment Florida turns. Bodies tethered to the ground as a news reel becomes the sky. I beg you, say anything on this couch in this house that's breaking down, locks fall from the doors, there are moments when everything moves in one direction and even us, unable to anticipate each other, even we are losing our foundation.

In the morning we go walking in Brighton. Disjuncture of autumn. Over soft shedding trees there is no sky. We walk past the library. You say it's another world. I say I don't know what to tell the women in my class tonight. We repeat *how* and *I knew it* as many times as we walk past the library.

Guard or protect someone or something from low temperature or inclement weather.

I repeat things, mistake things. I keep trying to build a house in my mind. It collapses and every interval of collapse breaks over us. If I listen, if I become a good wall, provide something for you—

We carry shorelines, inside jokes, burnt-out fields. We're born in the hollow after much has been lost. We carry memories that aren't memories but translations of things once said. What does it mean to hold? How is the candle lit inside so burning cold?

Proteger algo o a alguien de alguna amenaza cercana o peligro.

We're in a Dorchester writing room. Nothing can warm us. We craft questions from silence, peel silence down from the walls. The strips become words and it's like pulling repetitious scabs, wanting the blood to reopen.

Someone starts crying. Crying becomes a transferable state moving around the room, then you're the one crying. You say: *Este hombre es un monstruo, le falta humanidad.*

We're marked as less than human, so human things aren't for us. But if you dream of the place your humanity inhabits, you can touch and taste it and wonder if you could present these broken images as evidence to ICE.

Protect someone or something from a nearby threat or danger.

Broken images as evidence of humanity—painted door, pastel blue, adobe white, colores suavecitos the key, the potted orchid, the promise, the fig tree, a sunlit gate—

All this to say, I've belonged within a place. I had a mother who said *abrígate* at the slightest cold.

Children are being kept in the cold. The solar blanket was developed to deflect heat away from stations in orbit, then found to retain heat. Space forms between the body of the detained child and this new embankment. There are no echoes in the hollow.

Albergar o mantener una idea, deseo, o sentimiento.

In a chasm we're left looking up and waiting for wheat to drop from another's mouth. My sisters on the floor wrapping each other eternally. We can't stay this close, so are we less good to each other than a coat? Than the shelter of a dream?

Harbor or maintain an idea, desire, or feeling.

I dream of watching from an opposing treetop as my parents walk through the house they will buy, where they'll build our family. Azulejos under the fireplace. I watch Dad walk from room to room, see his smile and skepticism, and beg him not to enter the room where we will lose him. I beg a story not to happen.

In Tranströmer's "The Blue House," the dead repaint and rebuild walls and watch from the outside in. A line is drawn forward and backward in time. When I wear his coat it leaves my arms numb. Grief makes contact impossible.

My abuelita Emilia left Cuba with photographs stitched into the lining of her coat.

In some poems she's the archetype, *my grandmother*, and I'm sorry for the moments when even a slight step in language keeps you far.

Her abuelito would wake her too early so she could luxuriate in going back to sleep. He'd say, *para ti, oro molido,* for you, anything. She kept one memory of her father, how he laid a Band-Aid on her skinned knee in childhood. A tiny arch of care. Her mother stitched the name *Emi* into the sleeve where she kept her espejuelos and as she started to lose her memory she'd show me, how her hand, fragile with age, slid easily inside the shelter of her name.

All we know is what houses us, what tenderness speaks to us. The part of the lullaby that descends into melodic need. Possibilities of contact.

Poem for a Scorpion Child

Begin: a memory from before you can remember
much, the kind recounted to you so often
you've constructed it for yourself.

A woman came to the door. You watched
behind your father's legs. She wanted to sell
your house and you cried until she left.

Admit it: you were the child who cried too much. You
lacked a layer. You wanted to be a scorpion
but you weren't a scorpion.

You were whatever an exoskeleton protects.
Soft interiors.

Sol

You named me for light. How we belong
in the little spaces carved for us, love

tucking us into a walnut shell hollow
where you'd take the tiniest brush and paint
a Christmas star along the concavity—

Some days I'm a pendulum that exists on a planet
that periodically loses gravity. Some days

my light is spent, the light-years required
to travel back to myself too many.

Since you died I take tiny, redundant steps:
and, a, an. Articles on which I predicate
my survival.

I want to believe death is only a pause
in our continuous language. Stillness,

but what it means is cosmic change, that you and I
and the delicate spaces we drew into being

between us constitute a light source
that spears endlessly through a cloud break

as hope lances inside
            spherical borders.

Telephone Game

I spoke. You. Sound converted and delivered.
We smiled and spoke.

If we were closer, we say when we're apart.
If I tell you my body is full of stone caves
you understand the sadness there.

Words on an indirect path. Tell me where
we're going when we're not going anywhere.

Mimic me: this is a type of game.
Mimic me: este es un tipo de juego.

Dime a donde vamos, como es que nunca
vamos a ningún sitio. Las palabras empiezan

a girar. Si te digo que tengo el cuerpo lleno de
zarzas entiendes que hablo de una tristeza.
Si estuviéramos juntos ay si estuviéramos juntos.

Una luz convertida se entrega en mi cuerpo. Yo hablo. Tú.
Hablamos y sonreímos.

Semillas de lúcuma

Seed-pits lined up.
Each a word I learned
incorrectly

or not at all. Aquí
no se dice así.
Una fruta

típica de acá. Shred
texture. Days
punctuated by loss.

The right thing to
say or do as elusive
as a taste unremembered.

I always believed I
walked multiple
worlds but I lived

in pretranslation,
waiting for names to
drop into my mouth.

I'm sorry, a veces
me equivoco—

My slight and
rotating catalog
of apologies.

How to be an archive
of things no one
thought to tell?

With a Destructive Obsession

El aislamiento se instaló como la condición más común o más normal en nuestras vidas.
Recuerdo, con una obsesión destructiva . . .
    —Diamela Eltit

Receding, subordinating, I shifted
       into some corner of my brain

on a bed with the person who required
       I become that doll version of myself

in myself. [Exhale: I've placated them
       enough to avoid a fight.]

I like my shrunken
ascetic space. I become

a vitreous rod, my profile
linear.

Last week I said to you

      I used to eat twelve raw almonds for lunch   and you said

             in a day you'd eat only an apple.

Reflex-pressure. The texture of our smallness
      is shredded. In Eltit's *Impuesto a la carne*

a shriveled body exists in another, the mother inside
shrunken as if by internalized erosion.   A cavern inside the body

      builds its own wind patterns. A wound can eat me in reverse.

Algodones

Someone I love died
here, he died and I drove back
to Albuquerque. Days later,

another love, another death, a drive
back to Algodones to pick
up the ashes of the first.

I can't go farther than this.
On evening drives from Santa Fe I
repeat, I can't go farther than this,

not even within the earshot of my heart.

Barelyness of light. Windows
stud the juniper hills at dusk, catch
opposing sun. They become

containment fields I can't
reconcile. This place doesn't
mourn, there is no vigil, only

six small suns in the holding
of my throat.

Convento Santo Domingo

Hay un lugar lejos de toda ciudad.
   —Blanca Varela

Windows ring the bell tower.
Mourning, mouthing.

In a recreated room I write
letters to my dead, so Martín,
doctor who walked

through walls, might cross
solidities and find them.

The bell tower. Yellow archways
on oxidized black. I don't want
to climb the tower stairs. Some

certainty tells me I can't survive it, stairs
that present as exposed ribcage—

Lima from above. Rooftops
compile their own color, hide
their gray and their broken

light. A sun round with its edges
lost. Pink-and-yellow façades, balconies
built and rebuilt y ya llegamos a

la carretera donde uno se da
cuenta: I am apart from this city. Every
city. I am not who I am and maybe

this is vertigo, terror, I don't know
the history of that building, terror,
I can't map space, terror, teal,

yellow, brown a step away from
black. There is a place far

from all city. Not any city,
all. This is the translation.

Papi, Papá

I catch my head again.
I expect to see my father
entering a room. I catch
my head starting to turn

and I'm on the disappearing end
of an island, thinking of
the girl from El Salvador
whose sentences

are polite in a recording
from migrant detention.

They identify countries
of origin, not names. A crying
boy from Guatemala

says *Papi, Papi, Papá*. Dad, Daddy,
Father, I miss you. Please walk

through the door again.
Please inhabit your body.

Does he construct
a memory or a daydream

where his father, wearing the last
outfit he was seen in, enters
from the other side of a cage?

When I try to rebuild my father
it's his hair first, his shoulders, scenarios
of posture. I couldn't look at

the last thing he wore. I had
the chance I could not do it.

A child doesn't understand
separation. Absence is

transformed into a game: disappearance,
reappearance, a face
behind hands. I was there

the morning my father
crossed an undeniable border
and a boy is at the border now.

He catches his head
turning, looking

to the door and back, Papi,
Papá and the country beyond

the facility is desert and
wire and everything, everything

in this wide, cold
place is a pale-yellow polo,
tucked in at the waist.
A shirt his father wore.

Resuscitation

For a second: jackrabbit prints on snow and you're in the
frame again, lifting your arms to lower the sky for me.
On this side of Bridge Street we collect all the dead

sunflowers, cut rot from an amaryllis bulb
to end its dormancy.

Our box turtle wakes thin in spring. Asleep
all winter she witnessed

nothing. For a second small as a strawberry
all my dead are alive.

III

As if the story of a house
Were told, or ever could be

*Como si la historia de una casa
fuera contada, o pudiera ser*

—Edwin Arlington Robinson

Bird Sanctuary

. . . palabras que nos surgen de algún lado, como pájaros que huyen de nuestro interior, porque algo los ha amenazado.
—Alejandra Pizarnik

I have a poem in me tonight. Sounding out. Start of contact, wingtips to ribcage. It has nowhere to go but a fountain at the gates of a cemetery in Little Havana. How do I coax it to land there. How do I convince it yes, this is a safe place even though everyone here is dead. How do I get it to go where it needs. Release, release, no, don't escape back inside me, I may never get you close again. You need to breathe before I die. Your wings are weighed by something wet, blood or birth or refuse. Do you think I expected to give birth yet?

I expected my father to live to meet my children. He expected more—I'm sorry, I'm closing, a cage, I'm making it harder for you. What I want to tell you is that pain moves in two directions. My father who will not meet my children never knew where his own father was buried. It fractured him sometimes, that pain no longer bird, hardly recognizable as word.

But the cemetery where my grandfather is buried is a sanctuary for birds. So I want you to know you can go there, there will be no bone encircling you, that you if not me if not he will see all you could want, seed, sky, other birds, tissues left in trash cans, material for a nest.

Don't retreat, you're almost out, you've almost pierced, acute and localized. *Localizar* means I have identified the pain on a larger map. Look for the fountain and I will part like a promise for you. I will be strong enough to open.

The Blue Mimes / Los mimos azules

4 de julio: la costa verde

We turn the corner
and I see her

doubled over the seaside
bench in taut, iridescent blue.

Every movement slight: fingers
skim the ankle, head

angles up, shoulders
roll down. Her partner

approaches from
behind, teardrops half-painted

under his eyes. When
he walks he walks

stilted, a rhythm: Green coast.
Green coast. Gray water.

•

4 de junio: la casa

As a child I remember:
you kept a doll

in the annex window, staring
back into the main house to face

intruders, and in my mind
its yellow eyes fade.

Now I look out at twin
staircases as I sit

with you in my mother's
childhood bedroom.

There's no trash, so when
I hold your fingertips to clip
your nails I cup

the clippings too. We list
your brothers' names, even
the ones who have died and

I find that if I prompt you
to say my name as part of a list,

you're more likely
to remember it.

•

11 de junio

You're eating on a day
when eating paralyzes you.

Out the window: wires
crossed, the stained

profile of a half-finished house.
Pigeons huddle on

a clothesline, sway
according to the wind.

The man who buys unwanted
items from houses is calling,

a meditation in
his voice.

•

13 de junio

Música llega desde
la calle. Trato de no
pensar en esas

calles, acostumbrándome
ya a la callada.

•

15 de junio

Stained lace curtains. An in-between
zone from kitchen to

garden. Today we count
together the walled-off trees. Today
the inset door is locked.

My challenge: always find
space to occupy. I sit

on the annex stairwell,
looking back through windows

like an aged doll. Last night
you said *que sueñes con los*

angelitos pero por
la mañana no me acuerdo
si aparecieron o no.

•

19 de junio

It takes your fingers
so long to find the rim

of a coffee mug. They run
through a heap of clothes, rise

to the level of my face, spill,
cut, touch, stray. You fall

without warning. I think of
the boy in the market, dropping
his ball again and again

just to see who would
bring it back.

•

20 de junio

Memory is every side of you, the side
of your bed where light hits

in the morning when the door is left
open a crack, the way you expect

someone to be with you
when you wake and when

no one is there, it means
he must be waiting

for you on the black stone beach
where he played as a child.

We sit on a bench.
Across Avenida de la Marina,

the green light of a pharmacy.
We count hotel windows.

•

26 de junio

The privacy of your entrapment
is what terrifies me.

You search for your missing husband
under small objects, like a child

imagining that things and people can fit
where they can't, that you could

find someone by tugging
on a stuck drawer or rearranging

the wedding silver, and desperation
lies in believing that anyone

can be lost anywhere, that you
could search the same

couch cushions for months, or years.

•

1 de julio

You don't register
when I say I'm leaving.

Prométeme que no me vas
a olvidar–it's an impossibility,
but you respond, *nunca, nunca*.

•

2 de julio

The taxi parks outside
at 4 a.m. We're searching

for wedding rings, for things
we might have left in

wooden cavities littered
with bookworms.

As a child I remember a long ride
in the backseat, the last time

I left Lima: distant hunched
airport, light receding.

We couldn't fly out that day
and I had never been so long
from what I knew. I stared

out between driver and passenger
at musky yellowing lamps

and when we made it back to the house
through layers of coastal fog I eyed

my parents' wedding portraits as if
they were an entrapment.

•

4 de julio: la costa verde

Slow as gray water the driver
inches forward, pumping

his brakes while I internalize
the rhythm of chalk
white waves

and then we turn the corner
y la veo

agachada sobre un banco
vestida de azul tirante, iridiscente.

Cada movimiento fino: dedos
tocando el tobillo, cabeza

hacia arriba, hombros
hacia la tierra. Se acerca

su compañero, lágrimas
mitad pintadas debajo

de los ojos. Cuando
camina, camina rígidamente,

un ritmo: Costa verde.
Costa verde. Agua gris.

Naufragios

Does anything really
begin. The house, clinking
window frame in the last
of canyon wind. Does
anything begin.

•

The day a room becomes a field.
The day a field fills with water.
The day *you fall through yourself*—

this is how you say it—and how to respond to responses—

I'm sorry you capsized inside your body.
That must've been terrible—

•

Your left hand starts
swelling nightly. The body
now filled with unfamiliar and inflammatory substance.

You scratch until
skin scabs at three
lined-up points.

Orion's belt. Pinpoint self.
You're comforted by the symmetry
of your smallest wounds, how

you can keep scratching them open
and have a little composition
to keep you company.

This is only the surface of
the skin. Under moon,

the season's first monsoon
sequences the sky. Flash of rose.
Then begin the drenchings:

      pain salvage sink caveat absence—
they open and plunge into the depths of your body,
that system of caves.

•

It was so fast for you. How
did you catch your breath—

one after another you lost the people you loved as if they occupied
a single vessel and entered
the destructive radius of a storm.

Now nothing holds its water.
Nor its salt. Nor such heart.
Nothing has weight but everything
is an aspect of an unmovable weight.

•

There are parts of the ocean no natural
sunlight penetrates. In the basin

of grief you receive a dream where you try to distract the dead with inane conversation,
holding them but not long enough for them to realize they aren't meant to be anymore.

In the basin of grief these dreams
are the hanging light of an anglerfish.

Behind the contained, luminous target:
      a waking trap, and teeth.

•

You gather the memory-shatterings, the regret
you caught wandering your interior, the flakes
of scab that fill your selfsame

shipwrecked body. There are days you are the only
person who remembers there was ever ocean

in this desert, where the dampening
of fossils under rain becomes the only reminder
that everything lost was once alive.

Gray crests over a hill. Clouds in
thinning sheets, mountains black.

You become a field. Then
the air above the field.
Integration of wound and dark.

And one stone dislodges from
its burial sands.

The House It Is

June 2020

     Tonight you tunnel out of your skin,
burrow back in. You haven't gained
any new skills. Maybe

somewhere you are that
capable version of yourself.

            [But tonight you think of VHS Vivaldi, of winter wire-song played
            frenetic over footage of a forest somewhere,   somewhere forest,
            and as days morph deeper into heat you think you might be inside
            the wolf's awful taste in clothes: it looks like spring. It is the winter
            you lose everything.]

     In Lima, dolphins
repopulate la costa verde.

The same tides lapped
when you last stood

on those rocks, shadowed
water dark

as squid ink. Absence is playing, leaping,
reproducing. The way

ecosystems rebuild is too clean
       a metaphor for hope:

       in loss, gain, etc. no, we, horrible animal, lending the world back to itself.

            [In times of crisis the crisis learns to be locked at home with itself
            and its overly lucid dreams. Friend says her son's inability to express
            becomes the nightmare dragon whose weight is tactile. Yours is a sea
            monster: in the dream you sit on the pier outside La rosa nautica and

when the monster lifts its chameleon eye it lifts the world around you
to shattering.]

      The first day you walked out
to a changed charge, the light

of ending, of apocalypse
disbelieved. You projected

forward to the end of the year, the length of a line like the projected path of your run,
imagining

      how far you would have to go before
turning back to home-semblance.

      [Loose shopping carts in the grocery parking lot. Neighborhood dogs
      barking. Strained chorus of nothing at nothing at 6 p.m. The sky over
      I-40 painted into silence.]

When the cold comes you still won't be home.
When the cold comes you still won't be

with them, home. The composition is altered and this
      is the contention of grief: still a hole at the center

the hole you shaped with the intention of planting and no matter

how many masked trips you make to the nursery or
how many yellow tomatoes you stake,

the well remains a well.

      [The line between burial and growth. All this preparation
      for lost beginnings.]

      There is time, now, time
      spent filling time

with fortification, hoping
that ice really does trap heat

underneath. Gray-stained ice, little color. Who knew the cold could be

    a center, who knew we could cycle so many times
        a day inside ourselves,

bodies housing years
accelerated by worry.

    Now we must be attuned
to change. The flowering

of Spanish broom alters
the colorscape, blue

lavender thirsty today, so draining
and so young.

    Notice the color line where the stucco
    of the green townhouse and the terra-cotta townhouse

meet. This sameness, this minutely beautiful seam

from which miller moths
break in batches, archive it

the day you get the phone call: this virus
will take someone from you.

          [And while you slept there was also a car accident and
          you keep hearing that optimism is allowed because your
          beloved are feverless their chests are clear and the car's
          totaled but only her knees hurt. You keep hearing it, air
          that changes and becomes wind. Almost none of it reaches
          your lungs. Your body lunglike, molded to a bed.]

In a Sábato novel a house is described
in detail. You realize halfway through
a paragraph there's no window,

no door, no
> way to have entered, no way
> to leave.

You recognize your fear for the house it is
midway through the day, recognition
that lands like literary epiphany.

How much can change in the span of nothing changing?

[Some nights you want té de manzanilla in paper satchels,
the thing your mom associated with sickness. You drink it
as you walk the block alone, identifying, cataloging until
tea is cold. Back in the house, make sure the kitchen is
good, clean for tomorrow, the money transferred, the
flowers arrived in Surco, the best one can do. Some nights
you make a habit of reading and on the off nights wonder
if it really constituted a habit. Some nights outline a novel
in your head, others outline the course of a life until you
arrive at certain terror. Has anything changed. What about
the terror.]

[Days you map and remap the loop around the Manzano
open space, path encircling the abandoned foundation
of a house. Concrete steps split by lines of grass lead to
slabs like broken stages. Crack, scar, desert bleed. You
always thought something should happen here. Installation,
performance, Beckett, is it a tree or a shrub, is this where
we were meant to wait, all tumbleweeds arranged to look
like they're crawling. When the ruins lay such an even
groundwork, how can we resist the abandonment?]

When the ruins
lay
such an even groundwork

     the splitting foundation slides under each of us at once.

Brains of grass. A family
runs and laughs up a dirt hill, over
stones that spell BEEHIVE HOMES.

The earth rises and
the dolphins and
the wild grasses.

                      [You understand that you're given few possible actions in
                      the narrative of the movie, the dream, the novel structure,
                      the accident report, the imagined performance.]

    Tonight you are the one who examines your skin as a series of hills, who layers in
the text and fills the space reserved for a promise.

Birdsongs

Entonces, desde la torre más alta de la ausencia
su canto resonó en la opacidad de lo ocultado
en la extensión silenciosa
llena de oquedades movedizas como las palabras que escribo.
   —Alejandra Pizarnik, "Poema para el padre"

You were born with song in your mouth, a mastery of birds. Inevitable migratory life. Arrive at the day you told me stories of your migration and the terrible thing is I already forget, the fabric stretched and broken. A luxury high-rise across from the Habana Libre. Contracts with Lufthansa airlines. Your father at the national bank with Che, your father's miniature Minolta camera, your father, you.

We found letters between the two of you, written when you were brackets on either side of water. Elaborate puns woven into language. The father organizes the escape, cannot tell his son the details. The son, when he becomes a father, can only relay half-details while sitting in an art gallery with his daughter.

Your father. You. My father.

The gallery sells a spherical ceramic jar and a bird-shaped pipe holder and cans of beer. I forget the details. I remember I remember and I don't. Only the jar because we took it home, only the bird because we chose to leave it behind. I remember thinking the gallery was a beginning, that in the parting between branches you would start to speak until everything spilled out, a whole history unbraided. We would be whole.

If I rip open the bird, what happens. We recognize it's a pipe holder. We do nothing, elegantly. I hold the day when I cannot hold the detail. I am past and present tense when they resist clear delineation, there and here, sells and sold. I'm walking you back to the car you parked illegally. I rip the ticket off the windshield before you notice. The need for something to stay so perfect a twelve-dollar intrusion isn't allowed. Beginnings we don't know are denouement.

We make imaginary plans for Havana. Dream of meeting Leonardo Padura on a terrace somewhere. At home you point out the architecture of Havana schools in a Padura TV adaptation and show me walkthrough videos of the city on YouTube. Mauve balconies, juts of houses into the street, then someone turns a corner you remember. You pause, the image blurs. You say, this is where I walked with my dad.

Pipe tobacco, one of your smells. In my dreams I kiss your aftershave cheek and am I still the child who worried about your smoking after anti-smoking day at school or am I the adult who cradled the plastic bin of your pipe collection after you died and ran a thumb over the concavity of ash that still held something of you?

I know that you are you and sometimes you aren't. Sometimes you are the father, the son, the migrant, the archetype. I am walking a thin line of smoke. Parts of you so within me that I feel them radiating in my chest. Parts of you so far from that I can only conceptualize them as a half-understood, half-literary history.

Daily isolations. You didn't always understand our need to be not-alone. Family would go out for dinner, you'd head back early to be with the dog. How I had to drag you to that gallery. How talk of Cuba felt far because it was hard enough to get you to walk past the school grounds across the street. To remove you from your sphere of context. Retreat, retreat to where there is quiet and books and the story of a house.

My friend from Havana says all Cubans have this quality, como un sass, un humor, tu sabes. I ask if I have it. He laughs. He, at least, thinks I'm enough.

My understanding of an entire country came from a single person: you were Cuba to me. Watching the show, you'd say, that's it exactly, that's how everyone talks in Havana. That rhythm constituted a new language, like puns on typewritten paper.

I am you, sometimes you are you. This is all I know of collective identity.

First daughter, blue cap, impatient to exist. You were astonished by her smallness, held her in two hands the way you would hold and funnel birdseed. Curved detail of your head in hers.

Second daughter, I was almost born in the car. You could not have kept calm for that. When anything rose in you, terror, anger, panic, you would arrive at the same pitch, yelling at nurses, at the front desk, your tight command of language unraveling, those branches parting.

These are the partings that lead to spillage. An ink-dark fountain breaks, its water non-potable, something can't remain in the brain, can't remain in the mouth. Claws its way up the throat. The baby bird eats what emerges.

Third daughter shared your bird obsession. The two of you would stand outside in sunlight dappled by lilacs, pushing suet blocks behind little green rejas.

You would yell, we would leave. Distortion of tears. You would yell, we'd yell back, escalation until the space between us became electrical fire. You yelled. We were quiet.

But always we returned to each other, our collie between us in the backyard or laying his head on our feet in the kitchen. Arguments as unintended journeys: you'd travel into yourself, into your hurts, and in a vein of quiet you traveled back out. When you did, we were there to accept whatever book you placed in our hands.

You and I once translated a poem together. You were proud of an invention: *yawning pits* for *extensión silenciosa*. It referred to grief carved out, an emptiness left behind by a father who died too soon. You said the poem reminded you of your dad. One day it would remind me of you.

The father in the poem could never sing the song he was meant to, a song too symphonic for the containment of a life. Your father. You.

The song arrived to us braided from figures of speech. In the leftover story-pits, song. The song doesn't fit inside of a life but fits in the skull of a sparrow, sitting on a shelf in the gallery on our perfect day. A breakable thing, lacking its body, is still capable of sound. The slightness of air, threading through the gaps.

Fields Anointed with Poppies

1

I never thought of my body
as a shrine, but now

I feel the truth of its doors:
I carry the archaeology of you.

2

The day the world changed
sound, color, composition
at once the day the sky

inverted to become this
broken sheet—

the mountain, hanging
upside down, lost each one
of its golden poppies.

3

You were talking to me thirty minutes ago.

How am I supposed to learn now
to listen for you in wind, prayer language,
ghost tongue?

You were speaking to me thirty minutes ago.

4

Desire to be behind
a locked door. To be held, to be asked
after, to hate if the person asking lacks
the right words to hate words because
they lack totality. La profundidad.
La totalidad. Algo. Algo. To want
to be understood. To resist any claim
that anyone understands.

5

I listened to your last voicemail
again, the one about nothing. This time

it was hearing you say the word
tomorrow, an inflection so particularly

yours, as if the second O were wearing
a little hood of sound.

6

Hasta tenemos dos idiomas para decirlo: we have
two languages with which to approximate one pain.

Aguantar. Arrancar. Cataclysm. Fissure. *Cuídate*,
I said to you. I'll see you later today.

7

My mom asked if a memorial poem
had to be sad. Adjective with tiny wings.

Maybe a memorial poem is the way we
document the sky to each other, saying, look,

today the light breaks in five places and it is
so specific, so compositional, that it has to be
the person I lost the voice I lost the person

I lost speaking to me
in a new third tongue.

8

On an evening run I pass fields
anointed with poppies. A rabbit is

decaying where my route breaks
into desert and every day every
time I step over it, it is
a little less.

I am continuing past you.
The changes are changes
I have to catalog.

Every day lift new smells from the earth.
A little lilac. A little less.

And a road continues into open space.

Notes

The opening epigraph comes from "La noche de Santiago" ("Santiago Night") by Alejandra Pizarnik, published in *Prosa completa* (2001).

"Earthworks" and "The House It Is" were part of EKCO Poetry, a series of innovative, performative poetry projects by women, funded by Artful Life. I collaborated on this project with poets Valerie Martínez, Michelle Otero, and Rebeca Alderete Baca; we each wrote one poem in 2020, then another in 2021, documenting our experiences of the COVID-19 pandemic lockdown. We collaged those poems together into collaborative poetic documents. The 2021 collage, "A Day inside Ourselves," included fragments of "Earthworks" and was performed by myself, Michelle, and Rebeca in chorus as the opening ceremony for the virtual 2021 National Latinx Writers Gathering. Learn more about EKCO: www.artful-life.org.

"Earthworks" references the following land art installations by Andy Goldsworthy: *Sycamore leaves edging the roots of a sycamore tree* (2013), *Sumach leaves laid around a hole* (1998), and *Stone Coppice* (2009).

"Keys" was written in honor of women in transitional housing at the Brookview House in Dorchester, MA, who shared space with me in bilingual writing workshops in 2016 and 2017. This is the same workshop referenced in "Abrigar."

The epigraph to "multi-nights" comes from "Punk Half Panther" by Juan Felipe Herrera.

"The Split" references the aquatint *El sueño de la razón produce monstruos* (*The Sleep of Reason Produces Monsters*) by Francisco Goya (1799).

"summer at taos" was written in response to "Autumn at Taos" by D. H. Lawrence. It was written as part of my 2015 public art project, *Nerveless Taos*, in which the first line of each stanza was displayed on adobe walls in an alleyway in Taos, NM, as part of the 2015 PASEO arts festival. The letters were sculpted from carved wood, and the isolated lines created a mini-poem that could be read in two directions depending on which way viewers walked through the alley: "what we find / is a chasm of starlight / you & i / we pry open / what we once protected."

"Resound" contains a fragment from the song "Two-Headed Boy" by Neutral Milk Hotel. It was written in memory of my dear friend Isaac Sullivan-Leshin.

The first lines of "Quilla" echo the lines "hay una estrella azul al fondo de mi vaso / inagotable estrella / debe brillar en tus ojos cada vez que la miro" ("there's a blue star at the bottom of my glass / unquenchable star / it should gleam in your eyes each time I look at it"), from "Nadie sabe mis cosas" / "Nobody Knows What I'm Like" by Blanca Varela. The poem borrows imagery from myths of the Incan deity Mama Quilla (in Quechua, Mama Killa, or Mama-Kilya). Mama Quilla was seen as the calculator of the passage of time, the protector of women, the regulator of menstrual cycles, and the goddess of marriage. She was believed to cry silver tears. According to one myth, a fox fell in love with her and rose into the sky to pursue her. She pressed him against her, producing the dark patches on the moon. Lunar eclipses were seen as attacks on Mama Quilla.

"Sonnet to Sleep Paralysis" was written in response to John Keats's sonnet "To Sleep."

The epigraph for section II was written by my dad. It comes from his poem "The Laws We Broke," or "Laws," which won a poetry award when he was a student at Harvard. I also borrowed a line from this poem in "Telephone Game": "We smiled and spoke."

The line from Charles Baudelaire referenced in "Abrigar" comes from *Les paradis artificiels* (*Artificial Paradises*).

The definitions in "Abrigar" are quoted from *Oxford Living Dictionaries*, with my translation.

The lines "Some days I'm a pendulum that exists on a planet / that periodically loses gravity" in "Sol" refer to the novel *The Three-Body Problem* (三体) by Cixin Liu, translated by Ken Liu. In the novel, the extraterrestrial residents of the planet Trisolaris live under the threat of environmental collapse, caused by the planet's three suns. The gravitational forces of the suns repel and attract each other, which leads the planet's giant pendulums to swing erratically.

"Convento Santo Domingo" takes place at the famous convent in the historic center of Lima, which contains a recreation of the bedroom of San Martín de Porres. His attributed miracles include levitation, miraculous knowledge, instantaneous cures for the sick, and bilocation. It is said that during an epidemic that struck Lima during his lifetime, Martín would pass through locked doors to care for the sick, appearing in multiple places at once. Today, at the convent, visitors can write letters to loved ones who have passed away, with the hope that San Martín will pass through the veil of the afterlife and deliver the messages.

"Papi, Papá" references an eight-minute audio recording of migrant children crying out for their parents while being held in migrant detention at the US-Mexican border. The recording was obtained and released in June 2018, when government statistics indicated that nearly two thousand children were separated from their families over a six-week period between April and May.

The epigraph for section III comes from the poem "Eros Turannos" by Edwin Arlington Robinson.

The epigraph to "Bird Sanctuary" comes from an entry in Pizarnik's *Diarios* (2013 edition).

"The House It Is" references the novel *El túnel* by Ernesto Sábato (1948).

The epigraph to "Birdsongs" comes from "Poema para el padre" ("Poem for the father"), one of Pizarnik's uncollected poems. "Birdsongs" also touches on aspects of my paternal grandfather's story; my grandfather, Mario Lorenzo Rivera, worked as a CIA intelligence operative in the early 1960s, after working as an FBI intelligence operative in wartime munitions manufacturing throughout the 1940s. He was tasked with setting up a covert underground network to smuggle people to the US, while socializing with high-level revolutionary leaders in order to penetrate Castro's inner circle (in particular, he came to know Che Guevara well). He kept this double life secret until my dad, at fifteen years old, recognized his miniature Minolta camera as CIA issue after reading spy novels. At that point, my grandfather told my dad his entire story in one sitting.

"Fields Anointed with Poppies" was written for a community vigil event in Albuquerque in 2019, in which twenty-two poems were read to honor the twenty-two victims of the El Paso Walmart shooting. The poppies in the poem are the Mexican gold poppies of the Franklin Mountains.

The line drawings that act as section breaks for sections I and II were done by my dad. The line drawings in "Semillas de lúcuma" and on the book cover, as well as the section break drawing for section III, are my own.

Acknowledgments

Thank you to the following journals, anthologies, and digital platforms for publishing poems in this collection:

"Someone curls into themselves / Al borde del mar" published as text and video for La Maja Desnuda, 2022.

"multi-nights" in *Green Mountains Review*, Vol. 29, No. 2: Tribute Issue to PLOTUS Juan Felipe Herrera.

"The Split" in the *New England Review of Books*, July 2017.

"Poem for a Scorpion Child" in spoke 4.

"Sol" in *One Albuquerque, One Hundred Poems*, published by the City of Albuquerque (2022).

"Telephone Game" and "Resuscitation" in *236 Journal*, Issue 10, Summer 2021.

"Semillas de lúcuma" in *SeedBroadcast*, Issue 14.

"Convento Santo Domingo," "Algodones," and "Bird Sanctuary" in *Waxwing*, Issue XXVI, Winter 2022.

"Papi, Papá" in *The BreakBeat Poets Vol. 4: LatiNext* (Haymarket Books, 2020).

"The Blue Mimes / Los mimos azules" in *Solstice: A Magazine of Diverse Voices*, 2018 Summer Contest Issue, winner of the 2018 Stephen Dunn Prize in Poetry.

"Fields Anointed with Poppies" in *22 Poems & a Prayer for El Paso* (Dos Gatos Press, 2020).

"Quilla" in *Plume*, Issue 146, October 2023.

Thank you to Eduardo C. Corral for believing in this book enough to select it for this honor. Thank you for your continued kindness and support, and for helping me see my own work in new ways.

Thank you to the incomparable team at Graywolf Press for shepherding this book out into the world with such care. Thank you to my editor, Chantz Erolin, for your thorough, careful attention and feedback. Thank you to designer Mary Austin Speaker for your gorgeous work, and for giving me a chance to see my own drawings on the cover of this book.

Thank you to the Academy of American Poets for supporting debut books with such enthusiasm and generosity. Thank you to Jen Benka and Nikay Paredes for the best phone call of my life.

Thank you to the St. Botolph Club Foundation for funding this book in its early stages.

Thank you to my mentors: Amy Beeder, Diane Thiel, Robert Pinsky, Dan Chiasson, and Louise Glück. I will forever carry your lessons and your insights, all so deeply unique and varied, and I'll forever be grateful for the doors you opened for me.

Thank you to friends who read these poems and helped me understand all they could be, especially Valerie Martínez, Michelle Otero, Rebeca Alderete Baca, and Duy Đoàn. Thank you to Lisa Allen Ortiz for being my partner in translation; many of the Varela poems we translated influenced this book. Thank you to every friend who has ever formed part of my writing community, who has ever nourished my love of art and language.

Thank you to my causita, Kelly Vigil, for reading this book multiple times, and for the many years of writing, singing, and creating together that brought me to this point.

Thank you to my students. You fill my creative life with wonder and continuously shape my relationship to writing. Thank you to the organizations, institutions, universities, and community spaces that have invited me to teach, read, or speak, and connect with others over a shared love of words.

The memories of my beloved fill these pages. I owe so much of who I am to my abuelitos, whose love I felt constantly growing up, even across distance: Mario L. Rivera, Silvio Jova, Emilia Jova, Antonio Velásquez, and Adriana Velásquez.

Thank you to my mom, Ana Velásquez-Rivera, for modeling kindness, patience, and love to me my entire life. Thank you to my brilliant sisters, Alyssa Rivera and Gabriella Rivera; from co-authoring fantasy novels to poring over the lyrics of our favorite musicals, my obsession with language and stories began with you.

Thank you to everyone in my family who has ever shared their love of books with me, especially my tía, Silia Jova, and my prima and fellow poet, Adriana Miele.

Thank you to my husband, mi amor, Ian Alden, for the constancy of your support and love. The home we're building is filled with joy, safety, and laughter: the perfect foundation from which to create.

Thank you to my dad, Mario Rivera. When you taught me to draw, you taught me never to complete things too perfectly: it's the movement, the searching, that matters. In this book, I searched for you, searched for healing, and felt you with me, behind every word.

SARA DANIELE RIVERA is a Cuban Peruvian American artist, writer, translator, and educator. Her writing has appeared in *The BreakBeat Poets Vol. 4: LatiNext*, *Solstice*, *Waxwing*, and elsewhere. She lives in Albuquerque, New Mexico.

The text of *The Blue Mimes* is set in Sabon Next LT Pro.
Book design by Rachel Holscher.
Composition by Bookmobile Design and Digital
Publisher Services, Minneapolis, Minnesota.
Manufactured by Versa Press on acid-free,
30 percent postconsumer wastepaper.